D1382962

SCIENTISTS IN THE FIELD

ENTOMOLOGISTS

Robin Koontz

Rourke
Educational Media

rourkeeducationalmedia.com

Scan for Related Titles
and Teacher Resources

Before Reading:

Building Academic Vocabulary and Background Knowledge

Before reading a book, it is important to tap into what your child or students already know about the topic. This will help them develop their vocabulary, increase their reading comprehension, and make connections across the curriculum.

1. *Look at the cover of the book. What will this book be about?*
2. *What do you already know about the topic?*
3. *Let's study the Table of Contents. What will you learn about in the book's chapters?*
4. *What would you like to learn about this topic? Do you think you might learn about it from this book? Why or why not?*
5. *Use a reading journal to write about your knowledge of this topic. Record what you already know about the topic and what you hope to learn about the topic.*
6. *Read the book.*
7. *In your reading journal, record what you learned about the topic and your response to the book.*
8. *After reading the book complete the activities below.*

Content Area Vocabulary
Read the list. What do these words mean?

arthropods
conservation
diversity
ecology
ecosystem
habitat
herbicides
naturalists
pandemic
pollinate
taxonomy

After Reading:

Comprehension and Extension Activity

After reading the book, work on the following questions with your child or students in order to check their level of reading comprehension and content mastery.

1. *How do humans affect insects? (Text to self connection)*
2. *Why do you think there are still many insects and bugs undiscovered? (Infer)*
3. *What are pollinators and why are they important? (Summarize)*
4. *Entomologists are more than people who research bugs. They often specialize in different areas. Why do they need to specialize in specific areas rather than just one large field? (Asking questions)*
5. *Why would many entomologists enter the field of taxonomy? (Infer)*

Extension Activity

Insects, such as bees, are important to Earth's ecosystems. They help pollinate flowers and crops around the world. Think about the fruits and vegetables you eat and make a list. Research the items on your list to see if bees or other insects help create that food through pollination. How many foods did insects help create?

TABLE OF CONTENTS

FLYING FLOWERS

At a small field in Virginia, Dr. Lincoln Brower and his wife, Linda Fink, counted the delicate creatures perched on the bright pink flowers. They knew that the butterflies stopped to rest and eat as they traveled to their winter roosting sites. Lincoln wanted to help rescue these colorful orange-and-black butterflies.

The graceful creatures had amazed him for more than 60 years. He was not only impressed by the butterflies' beauty, but also by their amazing journeys. Monarch butterflies are the only butterflies known to travel up to many thousands of miles from North America to winter roosting sites. They fly to the mountains of Mexico, coastal areas in California, and other places far from their summer homes.

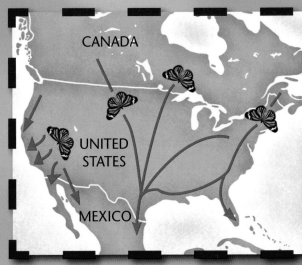

This map shows fall migration patterns of monarch butterflies.

A monarch butterfly lands on a milkweed flower.

The eastern population of monarch butterflies seems to like spending the winter months high above sea level. There, they can **hibernate** until spring. The oyamel fir forests in Mexico have just the right climate for monarch butterflies. It's cold, but not so cold that they must use their fat reserves to survive. The moisture from humidity helps to keep them healthy. And the trees are big and strong enough to support millions of butterflies as they gather for the winter. Some monarch butterflies fly as far as 3,000 miles (4,828 kilometers) to reach these special places.

Monarch butterflies on their way to their winter habitat rest on the pines and eucalyptus trees in Monarch Grove Sanctuary in Pacific Grove, California.

But in recent years, tourism and logging has taken away much of the monarch's winter **habitat**. And in the United States, their food supply has been depleted because of the use of **herbicides**. Scientists such as Lincoln know that monarch butterfly caterpillars only eat one thing: milkweed. Milkweed protects the caterpillars from being eaten by birds or other predators, because to them, milkweed is poisonous.

The brightly colored monarch butterfly caterpillars only eat milkweed. Their bright colors are a warning to predators that they are poisonous!

FIELD NOTES

The Mexican government recognized the importance of oyamel fir forests in 1986. They created the Monarch Butterfly Biosphere Reserve for monarch butterflies.

Milkweed was once abundant in the prairies across the Midwestern United States.

Milkweed used to be a common wild plant in the prairies across the Midwest. It continued to grow along with planted vegetable crops, but was considered a weed. Farmers sprayed milkweed and other plants with herbicides. In order to grow more crops, farmers developed herbicide-resistant seeds. They could now spread herbicides over a much wider area without killing the crops, too. With the loss of milkweed, monarch butterflies had no place to lay their eggs.

Lincoln believed that climate change was also affecting the survival of these creatures.

In 2014, Lincoln filed the first petition to have the monarch butterfly listed as threatened under the US Endangered Species Act. If the insects get the protection, Lincoln has more plans for them.

He wants land to be set aside for their food supply. He wants incentives for farmers not to put weed killer on all of their croplands. "Even if counties would just wait until after the frost to mow the roadsides that would make a big difference," Lincoln said.

And he hasn't stopped there. In order to track illegal logging in the roosting grounds, Lincoln formed a Geographic Information Systems team. Students and professionals from the University of Mexico, NASA, and Sweet Briar College work together to monitor logging activity. He also participated in **conservation** efforts to help local populations preserve and protect their forests where the butterflies roost.

The Center for Biological **Diversity** estimates that monarch butterfly numbers have gone from a billion to only 35 million in recent years. Their numbers seem to dwindle each year.

Each year, Lincoln traveled to the mountains in Mexico to view the millions of monarchs roosting in the trees. "You go in the forest and there are people with tears running down their faces," he said. "It's just so moving."

Lincoln is an entomologist. When people ask him why it should matter if we have monarch butterflies or not, it makes him angry. "That's just complete nonsense and a totally wrong way of thinking, but that's coming out as a biologist," he said. "That's why I am on this Earth."

FIELD NOTES

Monarch butterfly fans throughout the US planted milkweed in an effort to provide places for the monarchs to lay their eggs. But some of the milkweed was a tropical variety that didn't die back in winter in warm places such as the Gulf Coast. Milkweed can carry a parasite that weakens the butterfly. Normally the infected plants freeze and die in winter. But if the infected plant lives year-round, it can infect more butterflies.

WHAT IS AN ENTOMOLOGIST?

What's that bug? People often call anything that crawls on or around them a bug. And they sometimes want to squash it! Especially if it just bit them.

An entomologist studies all insects, including bugs. All true bugs are insects, but not all insects are bugs. All insects are **arthropods**. Entomologists may also study many other arthropods, such as spiders and scorpions.

Entomologists sometimes use an aspirator to capture small insects. They suck air through a tube while pointing another tube at the insect, which is then sucked into the vial.

Arthropods are different from all other animals because of a few special features. They have a skeleton on the outside of their bodies, called an exoskeleton. Their bodies are divided into distinct parts. For instance, an insect has a head, thorax, and abdomen. All arthropods have jointed legs and other appendages.

Arthropods include insects, arachnids, myriapods, and crustaceans.

FIELD NOTES

The key difference between true bugs and other insects is their mouth parts. True bugs have specialized mouth parts used to suck juices. Most of them suck fluids from plants, but there are some true bugs, such as bed bugs, that feed on humans and animals.

Insects have been around for millions of years. Insect ancestors may not look like today's flying or crawling creatures. One, the Meganeura, could have a wingspan of more than 30 inches (75 centimeters) and

According to the Smithsonian Institution's Department of Entomology, there might be 10 quintillion (10,000,000,000,000,000,000) individual insects alive at any one time.

weigh about a pound (450 grams). According to fossil records from 300 million years ago, the insect beast looked a lot like a very big dragonfly.

A cast of a Meganeura fossil shows how similar the ancient insect was to present-day dragonflies.

The history of entomology began with the study of animals in general. It wasn't until the 1600s that **naturalists** began to publish their discoveries and descriptions of insects. Entomology gained more recognition in 1745, when the first entomological society was formed in Great Britain. It did not have many active members for several years.

FIELD NOTES

Insects have been classified into 31 orders to date. For instance:

Moths and butterflies are grouped together in the order Lepidoptera, which means *scaly wings*.

Flies and mosquitos are in the order Diptera, which means *two wings*.

The order Hymenoptera, or *membrane wings*, includes ants and bees.

The largest order of insects is Coleoptera, or *hard wings*, which includes beetles and weevils. There are more than 300,000 species of Coleoptera in the world.

Illustrations of insects and other arthropods were once popular more as works of art than scientific study. There was no doubt that insects such as butterflies and bees were beautiful creatures that pollinated fruit and vegetable crops. There was also no doubt that insects such as locusts and many types of beetles damaged or destroyed fruit and vegetable crops. Other insects such as mosquitoes and fleas carried deadly diseases that killed thousands of people. Locating, identifying, and understanding all of these insects became some of the early tasks taken on by the first entomologists.

Weevils like this one can be a destructive insect both in its larval stage and as an adult beetle, feeding on everything from stored grain to cotton plants.

Entomologists use both aerial and sweep nets to collect insect samples. Aerial nets are lightweight for collecting flying insects.

Modern entomologists study everything you can imagine about insects and some of their relatives in the arthropod family. They study insect anatomy, habitats, their activity, life cycle, and behaviors. Entomologists also study how insects and bugs have evolved over time. They learn about insects' relationship to humans and the environment. Using their knowledge, entomologists research and help to design ways to control insect-borne diseases. Others come up with the best means to control and prevent crop damage done by insects.

Most entomologists discover new species of insects sometime in their careers. More than 900,000 species of insects have been identified. That means that insects make up about 85 percent of all known animal species. Entomologists believe there are many millions, perhaps even billions that they have yet to discover.

The many diverse jobs in entomology include research, teaching, **ecology**, agriculture, forestry, health and medicine, veterinary care, and even crime solving!

It's no wonder that these scientists have been fascinated with the most ancient, common, and diverse creatures on Earth since the first time one of the creatures flew through the air in front of them, crawled across their path, or bit them on the arm.

Sweep nets are more heavy-duty to drag through dense vegetation.

While photography is widely used to capture images of insects, entomologists still find illustrations useful. Scientific drawings can sometimes more accurately illustrate parts and features.

The Smithsonian Institution in Washington, D.C. has more than 126 million specimens of animal life, including more than 35 million insects. It is the second largest collection in the world. Collecting and preserving insects and other creatures help scientists to identify and understand each one. Specimens are studied and preserved for future scientists. Many entomologists enter the field of **taxonomy**, which involves the classification of organisms.

RESCUING NATURE'S POLLINATORS

Pollinators are a vital part of the Earth's **ecosystem**. Pollination is what makes a plant produce seeds. Insects **pollinate** close to 90 percent of our flowering fruit, nut, and vegetable crops. And about 80 percent of those pollinators are honeybees, both wild and domestic. One colony of bees can pollinate about 300 million flowers in a single day.

Grain crops, such as wheat, are pollinated mostly by the wind. But most other human food crops rely on bees. Without these pollinators, people in many parts of the world would have little to eat.

Honeybees have been dying off in recent years. A worldwide colony collapse accounted for massive honeybee losses. The worker bees suddenly abandoned their hives, causing the colonies to perish.

When a bee feeds on the pollen and nectar from a flower, its bristled body picks up pollen. The bee then spreads the pollen to the next flower it visits.

An apiary is a place where honeybee hives are kept.

Entomologists who study honeybees are called apiologists. They recognize that many factors can cause honeybees to die. Drought and a lack of food are reasons. Air pollution and climate change can also be to blame. But the biggest problems appear to be pesticides, parasites, and habitat loss.

Cutting down trees and developing wild areas for construction or farming can harm the native species that thrive there.

Maryann Frazier is an entomologist and a senior extension associate at Penn State University. Their research station is called the Wiley Apiary. Maryann and a team of researchers study the ways pesticides hurt honeybees and other pollinators.

They've discovered through shared data that often many kinds of pesticides can be found in a single colony. Since bees can travel several miles on daily forages, they can pick up all kinds of chemicals as they gather pollen from different flowers or pass through spraying operations.

FIELD NOTES

Apiology is the scientific study of honeybees. It is a subdiscipline of melittology, the study of all bees, which is a subdiscipline of entomology.

"It was pretty shocking to us, when we looked at a spectrum of colonies across the country, the diversity and levels of pesticides that we were seeing coming into honeybee colonies," Maryann noted.

They've discovered that a lot of exposure to pesticides can shorten a bee's lifespan. It can also affect how the bee communicates, flies, and locates and collects food. Worker bees suffering from pesticide exposure can affect the health of the entire colony.

Broadcast spraying of pesticides and herbicides to protect some food crops can create long-lasting damage to the ecosystem.

Pesticides also have inert, or inactive, ingredients. These ingredients are not disclosed, and often they are not regulated. The researchers are concerned that some of these ingredients might also have a negative impact on honeybee health.

For testing, Maryann and her team create a young colony of bees that are treated with pesticide. Sadly, they have to sacrifice bees in order to examine the impact of the chemicals.

"It's very hard," Maryann said.

But they know that the study is done to help all bees. Without pollinators, the world would change. An entire ecosystem would lose an important participant. In time, their loss would affect almost every living thing, including humans. So, Maryann and her team observe how long one generation lives after exposure to the pesticide. The team studies other issues that could also be killing bees, such as parasites. But their primary goal is to find out what we can do to keep the bees alive.

In 2014, the president of the United States created a "Federal Strategy to Promote the Health of Honeybees and Other Pollinators." A Pollinator Health Task Force was set up. It is headed by the Environmental Protection Agency (EPA) and the US Agriculture Department (USDA). Their job is to identify ways to work to stop and prevent the growing loss of honeybees and other pollinators.

DISEASE DETECTIVES

Throughout history, insects have bitten humans and animals and sucked their blood. The Black Death was a plague **pandemic** that swept through Asia and Europe, killing possibly as many as 25 million people. It wasn't until the late 1800s that researchers thought they figured out what caused this horrible disease that kept reappearing throughout history. They discovered that rats were also getting sick from the plague, and that infected people had flea bites. The flea was the disease vector, and rats, along with other mammals, were the carriers. Later, in 2014, it was discovered that gerbils, not rats, were the main plague-spreading suspect.

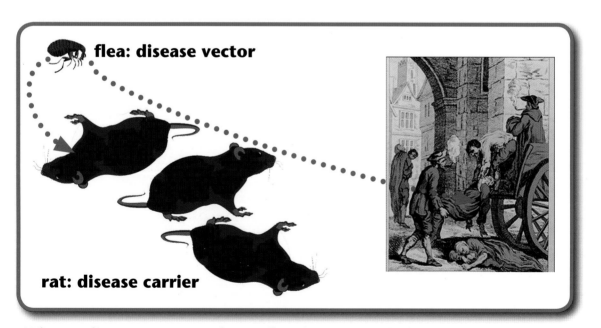

flea: disease vector

rat: disease carrier

When a disease vector, such as a flea, bites something, it transmits the disease through its bodily fluids.

A bacteriologist named Theobald Smith discovered that ticks can transmit diseases such as Texas cattle fever. His findings gave other scientists clues about another blood-sucking insect, the mosquito. Mosquitoes probably cause more diseases and deaths than any other organism. They can spread malaria, yellow fever, and West Nile virus to humans as well as other deadly diseases. Malaria kills about a million people each year. Mosquitoes are also the vectors of dog heartworm and equine encephalitis as well as other diseases that are harmful and often deadly to pets and livestock.

Theobald Smith
1859-1934

A tick's specialized feeding appendage is armed with sharp structures that it uses to slowly burrow its way into skin.

Many entomologists decide to specialize in the medical or veterinary field. They study fleas, ticks, and mosquitoes as well as lice, mites, parasites, and any other organism that has the potential to transmit diseases to people or domestic livestock and pets. They might also study the diseases to figure out how they spread and if there is a disease vector at work.

Dr. Nina Stanczyk is a research fellow in medical entomology. She has spent much of her career studying mosquitoes and malaria. She knows that a good way to prevent the spread of malaria and other mosquito-borne diseases is not to get bitten! One of her studies was about tricking mosquitoes' sense of smell.

"I look at manipulating mosquito behavior. How? I look at what makes the mosquito respond in a certain way and see if I can use that against it," Nina says.

A female mosquito probes around under the skin until she finds a blood vessel.

Since mosquitoes track us down by using our odors, Nina set out to discover the smells they are most attracted to. On a typical day for this particular study, she collected some female mosquitoes from a special containment area. The mosquitoes were isolated because they were fed a meal of malaria parasites.

She compared their behavior with uninfected mosquitoes. One test was to put a sock on a cage and see how many mosquitoes bit it. Mosquitoes love human foot odor! Nina also tested brain signals, a very tedious task. She hoped her research would tell what odor could be used in mosquito traps that could attract and snag the ones carrying the deadly malaria disease.

Mosquitoes and other insects detect body heat, carbon dioxide from breath, and odors. Repellent sprays keep insects away by confusing their odor receptors.

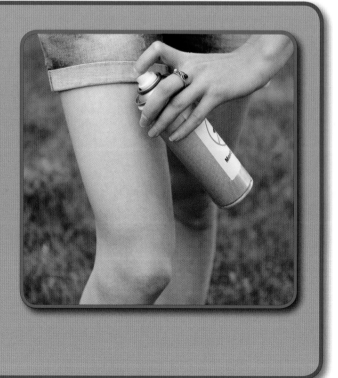

Nina was also involved in research that discovered mosquitoes are actually drawn to malaria. In the study, they were attracted to mice that were recovering from the disease. The researchers knew that the parasite would be at high levels at the late stage of malaria.

Somehow, the parasite altered the mouse's odor, making the mosquitoes want to bite it. This information could help identify human carriers by screening them for the special chemical scent that attracted mosquitoes. These people could then be isolated and treated.

With millions of people and animals getting sick or dying from insect-borne diseases, the work these entomologists do and the discoveries they make are extremely valuable to us all.

FIELD NOTES

The Division of Vector-Borne Diseases (DVBD) was set up by the Centers for Disease Control and Prevention (CDC). Its goal is to protect the US from diseases that are spread by mosquitoes, ticks, and fleas.

Only female mosquitoes bite, but it's not actually a bite. It pokes with a proboscis and finds a blood vessel. It injects saliva that works to make the blood thin enough to suck. It is the mosquito's saliva that can contain malaria parasites, bacteria, and viruses. This is how the pesky insect transmits all those deadly diseases.

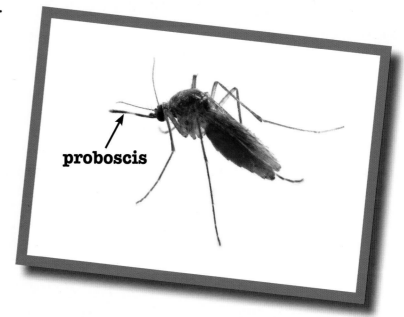

proboscis

COMPOSTERS AND MINI-DETECTIVES

Insect pollinators make sure plants survive by helping them to seed. But insects also take care of plants after they die. Many kinds of insects and arthropods chomp through dead plants, trees, animal waste, and dead animals. This is part of a process called composting. Composting is nature's way of recycling decomposed organic materials into a nutrient-rich soil known as compost. That soil in turn nurtures new life.

Ants, millipedes, mites, centipedes, sowbugs, springtails, flies, spiders, and all kinds of beetles consume dead stuff. Bacteria, fungi, snails, slugs, and worms also contribute to the composting process. Many organisms involved in composting are microscopic animals.

Centipedes have claws in the first pair of legs that they use to inject poison into their prey, usually insects and spiders.

leaves,
woody materials

grass, food scraps,
manures

compost

water

air

compost
happens

macro-organisms
(earthworms, insects, etc.)

micro-organisms
(bacteria, fungi, microbes)

For gardeners, a good compost pile not only takes care of kitchen scraps, it becomes soil for next year's vegetable crop. Gardeners may not know about all the creepy composters or just what goes on inside a compost heap. They do know that the end result is soil that can be put back in the garden.

One of the insect heroes of composting is the black soldier fly. At a farm in Georgia, this insect has become a welcome addition to the farm's zero-waste goals. The fly doesn't bite, and is not known to carry any diseases. That's good news, but the better news is that the fly larvae are master composters. They can turn a manure heap into a pile of soil. And the larvae are also an excellent food source for the chickens!

The farmers decided to raise the flies, and they put Lori Moshman in charge. Lori has a background in entomology. She consulted with entomologist and black soldier fly expert Craig Sheppard for extra help. Her goal was to design a good way to raise black soldier flies for composting animal and crop waste, and for chicken feed for the farm's 90,000 chickens.

black soldier fly

Insects as Clues

Dr. Amoret Whitaker also worked with insect composters, specifically those that consume dead bodies. She removed them from the body and studied them under a microscope. Then she kept the creatures in incubators to find out how far along they were in their life cycle when they were removed. The age and species of the insects and their larvae gave Amoret a timetable of when the person died.

Blowfly larvae called maggots are excellent body composters.

Forensic entomologists such as Amoret have a job that few people want to think about. But understanding and measuring the life cycle of insects as they work to decompose a body can be a big help to police. Their work helps authorities solve crimes.

Amoret had a lab, called the Insectary, on top of one of London's Natural History Museum's gothic towers. The museum managers kept her and her work up there because they said that it smelled bad. Amoret once said, "I thought I'd end up working with big furry animals like polar bears or gorillas. But then I saw insects under the microscope and realized how complex and fascinating they are."

Natural History Museum, London

Amoret also talks to students to share her passion for forensic entomology. "I try to show them that I'm a scientist doing something exciting [and] useful to society," she said.

FIELD NOTES

Insects tend to stick to a certain area. Forensic entomologists can study bugs captured in a car grill to figure out where the driver traveled. Even mosquitoes can be useful in a crime investigation. The blood they suck can contain DNA that identifies a person. The entomologist traps mosquitoes at the crime scene and sometimes can find evidence of who was there at the time of the crime.

Blood collected from a mosquito can be tested to identify where it came from.

UNDERSTANDING THE BAD GUYS

Termites eat the cellulose in wood as well as in cardboard, paper, and other plant material.

We know that insects are beneficial in many ways. We also know they can be harmful by spreading disease and causing food shortages. There are also insects that cause massive crop damage, destroy entire forests, and even invade our homes and businesses. Some of them devour the buildings that we live in. One of the biggest challenges entomologists face is controlling the bad guys. There is an important calling for entomologists to work in insect pest research and management.

Historically, people have introduced all kinds of pesticides with results that have sometimes backfired. They often found that when they killed the insect pests in an area, they also killed the natural predators. And guess what? The pests returned, immune to the pesticide and free of threats from their natural enemies, because their natural predators were gone. Entomologists try to find the best ways to use pesticides. To do that, they have to research and try to understand the insects that cause so much destruction in our lives.

The US ban on a pesticide called DDT and the implementation of the Endangered Species Act were major factors in the comeback of the bald eagle, scientists say.

One potential bad guy is a grasshopper relative called a locustidae, or locust. Their natural activity is to swarm during one phase of their life cycle. If the conditions are right, they can group into gigantic, hungry swarms that devour everything in the way. One swarm can have up to 80 million locusts in less than half a square mile (one square kilometer).

The swarm can be 460 square miles (1,200 square kilometers) in size, nearly as big as the city of Los Angeles. And each locust can eat its own weight in plants in one day. Locusts can cover vast distances during one of their devastating swarms. Their swarms have caused massive damage to agricultural crops in large parts of Africa, Asia, Central and South America.

Dr. Greg Sword, professor of entomology at Texas A&M University, led an international team of entomologists and other scientists in an amazing project. They used computer simulations to better understand locusts' destructive nature of swarming. The study helped them observe how and when these normally calm creatures can turn into voracious eaters when gathered in a crowd. Locusts are normally pretty shy and solitary animals. But in just a few hours, they can become a riot of eating machines.

One locust swarm can cause widespread famine and starvation throughout the affected region.

The computer modeling was able to describe real locust behavior that would usually be seen in nature. What the scientists discovered was that the locusts were not focused on eating plants. They were mostly trying to escape other locusts! For some reason, during this phase, called a gregarious phase, the locusts behave like cannibals, eating other locusts. And unfortunately, in the process, they eat whatever plants are around along with their neighbors.

Greg noted that stopping the crazed locusts before they began to swarm might prevent the massive destruction before it begins. Before locusts swarm, flightless juveniles gather and migrate as a mass march. This could be the best time to stop the swarm.

When juvenile locusts gather in a group, their behavior starts to change from calm to more active.

This study and others that use computer simulations help farmers manage a possible onslaught of locusts. They might know better where, and when, to apply pesticides.

"If we can tell when and where to most effectively place pesticides, this will help cut down on costs and the environmental implications. It is a win-win situation." Greg said.

Entomologists work to find ways that humans and insects can live together in harmony. These scientists know that messing with the Earth's ecosystem can have devastating results. Whether we like it or not, insects are here to stay. And that is a good thing.

If you can't beat them, eat them. Two entomologists and a chef published *The Insect Cookbook: Food for a Sustainable Planet.* They say insects can be a good source of protein for humans. One of the authors is a consultant on insects as food for the Food and Agriculture Organization of the United Nations.

Want to get involved? There are many ways you can help in the entomology field as a citizen scientist.

Monarch Watch: Help with the Bring Back the Monarchs Campaign and check out fun activities for kids.
www.monarchwatch.org

Bumble Bee Watch: Help researchers study bumble bees and help with their conservation, upload photos and learn about bumble bees.
www.bumblebeewatch.org

The Great Sunflower Project: Join the program and get ideas for growing flowers that help the pollinators.
www.greatsunflower.org

Dragonfly Pond Watch Project: Observe dragonflies at local ponds and share the information.
www.xerces.org/dragonfly-migration/ pondwatch

Firefly Watch: Map fireflies found in New England and beyond, just by hanging out in your backyard or local park on warm summer evenings.
https://legacy.mos.org/fireflywatch

TIMELINE

Aristotle (384-322 BCE): His book, *History of Animals*, included insects in a class called Entoma.

Ulisse Aldrovandi (1522-1605): He published *Of Insect Animals* in 1602.

1745: The first entomological society was formed in Great Britain.

René-Antoine Ferchault de Réaumur (1683-1757): He published the first of several volumes called *Memoirs Serving as a History of Insects* in 1734. Though it was never finished, his memoirs were a milestone for entomology.

Pierre-André Latreille (1762-1833): He was credited for the first detailed classification of insects and crustaceans. He is often considered to be the father of modern entomology.

Thomas Say (1787-1834): He was a naturalist considered to be the founder of descriptive entomology in the US. He was the first to describe more than a thousand of our familiar insects.

Charles Valentine Riley (1843-1895): He helped establish the Division of Entomology of the US Department of Agriculture. He helped make farmers aware of the importance of insect control for their crops.

John Henry Comstock (1849-1931): His studies of scale insects, butterflies, and moths became the basis for classifying these insects.

Frank Eugene Lutz (1879-1943): He was one of the first American entomologists. He set up experiments that studied heredity based on the lives of the common fruit fly. He is the author of the classic book on insects, *Lots of Insects*.

Karl von Frisch (1886-1982): He was a zoologist who discovered how honeybees communicate by dancing.

1889: The Entomological Society of America (ESA) was founded. It is now the largest organization in the world that promotes entomologists and related studies.

WAYS TO GET IN THE FIELD

Entomology could be the career for you if you are fascinated by insects. A field guide to insects and a magnifying glass are good tools to get started. An important discovery could be made right in your own neighborhood! Visit museums and read bug books. Keep a journal and make sketches of the arthropods you see, or take photographs and create your own album of creatures.

Glossary

arthropods (AR-thruh-pods): animals without a backbone that have a hard outer skeleton and three or more pairs of legs that can bend

conservation (kon-sur-VAY-shuhn): the protection of valuable things, especially natural resources

diversity (di-VUR-suh-tee): variety

ecology (ee-KOL-uh-jee): the study of the relationship between plants, animals, and their environment

ecosystem (EK-oh-siss-tuhm): a community of animals and plants interacting with their environment

habitat (HAB-uh-tat): the natural place where a plant or animal lives

herbicides (HUR-buh-sides): chemicals that destroy plants, usually weeds

naturalists (NACH-ur-uh-lists): people who study animals and plants

pandemic (pan-DIM-ik): widespread disease epidemic

pollinate (POL-uh-nate): to carry or transfer pollen from the stamen to the pistol of flowers

taxonomy (tak-SAN-uh-mee): the science of classifying organisms

Index

Show What You Know

1. What are three things that are causing monarch butterflies to disappear?
2. What creatures do entomologists study that are not insects?
3. What are some ways that honeybees can be saved?
4. What is meant by the term "zero-waste"?
5. What ways can a computer be used to study insects?

Websites to Visit

www.amentsoc.org/bug-club
http://kids.sandiegozoo.org/animals/insects
http://animals.nationalgeographic.com/animals/bugs

About the Author

Robin Koontz is a freelance author/illustrator/ designer of a wide variety of nonfiction and fiction books, educational blogs, and magazine articles for children and young adults. Her 2011 science title, *Leaps and Creeps - How Animals Move to Survive,* was an Animal Behavior Society Outstanding Children's Book Award Finalist. Raised in Maryland and Alabama, Robin now lives with her husband in the Coast Range of western Oregon where she especially enjoys observing the wildlife on her property. You can learn more on her blog, robinkoontz.wordpress.com.

Meet The Author!
www.meetREMauthors.com

© 2016 Rourke Educational Media

www.rourkeeducationalmedia.com

PHOTO CREDITS: Cover: main photo © Valeriy Kirsanov | Dreamstime.com, beetle photo © irin-k/shutterstock page 4-5 © csterken, butterfly on map © Butterfly Hunter, map © KPG_Payless; page 6 © Anatoliy Lukich; page 7 (and throughout) notepad © iunewind, page 7 © Cathy Keifer; page 8 © Ken Schulze; page 11 © © Valeriy Kirsanov; page 12 © Mirek Kijewski, PanStock, Denis Vrublevski, avarand; page 13 © Hcrepin; page 14 moth © Jiri Hodecek, fly © irin-k, bee © Peter Waters, beetle © bluehand; page 15 © skydie; page 16 © © Igabriela; page 17 © Valeriy Kirsanov; page 18 top left © dimitris_k, top right © Kondor83; page 19 single bee © pixel, bee on flower © Tsekhmister; page 20 © Steve Oehlenschlager; page 21 top left © American Spirit, top right © Jeffrey B. Banke; page 22 © Denton Rumsey; page 24 rat and flea © ottoflick, page 25 © PHOTO FUN; pages 26-27 © xmee, page 28 © Africa Studio; page 30 © Imfoto; page 31 © Imfoto; page 32 leaves © Alexander Kazantsev, food scraps © Mona Makela, compost bucket © Sarah Marchant, earthworm © Maryna Pleshkun, fungi © Kichigin, water and air icons © Vectomart; page 33 © paulrommer; page 34-35 © TimVickers; page 36 © pious, page 37 © Henrik Larsson; page 38 © Peter Kai, page 39 © Phillip Rubino; page 40-41 © © Paweł Opaska/Dreamstime; page 42 © Zumaandme/Dreamstime; page 43 © D. Kucharski K. Kucharska; page 44 icons © Cube29

Edited by: Keli Sipperley

Cover and Interior design by: Nicola Stratford   www.nicolastratford.com

Library of Congress PCN Data

Entomologists / Robin Koontz
(Scientists in the Field)
ISBN 978-1-63430-410-8 (hard cover)
ISBN 978-1-63430-510-5 (soft cover)
ISBN 978-1-63430-602-7 (e-Book)
Library of Congress Control Number: 2015931710

Printed in the United States of America, North Mankato, Minnesota

Also Available as:
ROURKE'S **e-Books**